New Dark Ages

Other books
by Donald Revell

From the Abandoned Cities
The Gaza of Winter

New Dark Ages

Donald Revell

Wesleyan University Press
Published by
University Press of New England
Hanover and London

The University Press of New England

is a consortium of universities in New England dedicated to publishing scholarly and trade works by authors from member campuses and elsewhere. The New England imprint signifies uniform standards for publication excellence maintained without exception by the consortium members. A joint imprint of University Press of New England and a sponsoring member acknowledges the publishing mission of that university and its support for the dissemination of scholarship throughout the world. Cited by the American Council of Learned Societies as a model to be followed, University Press of New England publishes books under its own imprint and the imprints of Brandeis University, Brown University, Clark University, University of Connecticut, Dartmouth College, University of New Hampshire, University of Rhode Island, Tufts University, University of Vermont, and Wesleyan University.

Some of these poems appeared originally in *The Agni Review, Antaeus, Boulevard, The Missouri Review, The New Republic, Pequod, Ploughshares, Shenandoah, Sulfur,* and *Willow Springs.* "The Northeast Corridor," "1848," "1919," "Survey," "How Passion Comes to Matter," and "Apocrypha" (as "The World") were first published in *The American Poetry Review;* "St. Lucy's Day," "Psalmist," and "The Night Orchard" in *Poetry.* "St. Lucy's Day" also appeared in *Best American Poetry 1988.*

The author would like to thank the National Endowment for the Arts for a grant that helped to make the completion of these poems possible.

Printed in the United States of America

♾

Library of Congress Cataloging-in-Publication Data

Revell, Donald, 1954–
New dark ages / by Donald Revell.
p. cm. — (Wesleyan poetry)
ISBN 0–8195–2184–1 : $18.00. — ISBN 0–8195–1186–2 (pbk.) : $9.95
I. Title. II. Series.
PS3568.E793N4   1990   89–49759
811'.54 — dc20   CIP

WESLEYAN POETRY
5   4   3   2

For Carson, My Daughter

Contents

I

Si recte calculum ponas,
ubique naufragium est.

—Petronius Arbiter

Survey

I am so lonely for the twentieth century,
for the deeply felt, obscene graffiti
of armed men and the beautiful bridges
that make them so small and carry them
into the hearts of cities written like words
across nothing, the dense void
history became in my beautiful century.
When a man talks reason, he postpones something.
He gets in the way of a machine that knows him
for the sad vengeance he is, somewhere close
to the bald name of his city. "New York"
means "strike back." "Attica" means "strike back"
and so does any place in the world
in the huge eyes and tender hands of my century.

I went to the capital. I had a banner
and there were thousands of people like me.
There was an airplane, and for a moment
heavy with laurel and sprays of peach blossom
something that had never happened before
stretched like a woman's shadow on a hedge
between the plane and the people who saw it flying.
It was the real name of the century.
It told everyone to strike back
until there was no reason in the world
except a machine stalled overhead
that knows everyone and is as delicate
as peach blossom. But the poor years come too late.

1848

Uneven sounds whiten the pavements
after nightfall. The tall hats of rebellion
have taken on a life of their own,
floating and rearranging tirelessly
over the pavements of the old streets
which by 3 AM are white as bones.

Every hour of my sleep is a useless rebellion.
I dream that you return to hear one last
argument, to touch my face in the hallway
a last time before the interdiction,
the yellow bulb between apartments
sputtering like a bad kiss as you go.

Justice demands that no one be loved for himself.
Freedom demands that each kiss be a contract
between desire and the unformed constellations
of all objects—whatever is dreamed,
whatever is stolen from the thief of possession,
whatever strikes the bone of pavement

as a woman steps out of a tenement
into the permanent rebellion
of which she is blameless. In 1848
the social contract becomes a horrid loneliness.
Justice abandons freedom and freedom
begins to think of itself as a new star,

a light in a hallway and then a thousand lights
careering over the bones of uneven pavement.
When I lie down in bed tonight
I will think of a new argument
to turn the tide of rebellion against freedom,
to press hands to faces until they touch bone.

How Passion Comes to Matter

When I was a boy, my father drove us once
very fast along a road deep in a woodland.
The leaves on the trees turned into mirrors
signaling with bright lights frantically.
They said it was the end of the world and to go faster.

I am beginning to know in whose name
the uprisings, the sudden appearances
of facades like damp cloths, somehow happen.
Think, for me, of a woman thrown
in front of a train. You can see her

falling in the staccato of her last gesture,
that little wave, and she will never stop
leaving you, just as you will never find
a kiss that can move faster than a train.
Or think, rather, of a boy

who felt the death inside his first lover
and went home and died of gunshot in his sleep.
I know there is a cult of such things—the young dead.
I understand the excess they cause.
But as passion is their signature, admit

we are grief-sodden and thus romantic.
We raise no columns in the great style but only
the anxious facades of left-wing cities
never to be completed. She brings
a damaged son and an open mouthful of milk

to one who is always leaving her and she
reappears suddenly under the low and inwrought
housefronts of April, that month teeming
with slaughter. It is the pause of the world.
Time triumphs in an incompleteness we can feel

on each other's bedding. In the unstill noise
of couples, high, shameless operas prove
the truth of uprisings, guiltless trains, gunshots
in a boy's sleep. Father drove us very fast.
In left-wing cities, we can drive no faster.

1919

All that year, the fronts of houses
wore the faces of rebel angels
and eyes draped with the figures of human bodies
in the attitude of a dance,
the dancers' limbs curved like lemon flowers.

The palace was a keyboard instrument.
The cafes floated on early snow
and the boulevardiers eddied like yellow petals
in the whorls of snow between the tables.
In that year, each mouth kissed your neck

with a damp flutter, almost too softly.
I need to go backwards that far to see
the faces of the last actors
aware of no difference between aspiration
and silliness, hope and kitsch.

People end up with one another.
The sex is terrible, or the sex is nothing.
Late, with a metropolitan lateness,
couples lower the eyes of their freedom,
and a brief, annihilating music

reminds them in narrowing whorls, so many
useless futures and a passion
nearly to bite through handcuffs.
I like earliness and the feel of the provinces.
I love the wonderful year 1919

and daring housefronts newly scrubbed
postered with slogans announcing
no need to be ashamed of hope,
no limit to aspiration which is to be shared
with the actor on your right hand

and a dazzling sequence of actors—
sky, drapery, and the human figure—on your left.
But people end up with one another in great cities.
I get up late, and since she is still sleeping
I go out. The buildings say only

that they have seen over the stele of the future
and stand guard against the emptiness there
because I could not bear it.
In 1919, men and women stood at the height of buildings.
They played upon each other as upon keyboard instruments.

Psalmist

The first thing out of the harp is sky.
The second is the art of dance
as practiced in front of all Jerusalem,
all the people brought into one city,
and a small boy at the edge of the crowd
loses his heart just seeing their faces.

Suddenly, we find the power of charity.
It is what I cajole out of myself
and shape onto your face like a crude face—
clumsy spirals and a warm look
under bedclothes. It sets people writhing
like sexy reeds in a lake's applause.

The power of charity is the guilty numbers.
I give myself, and that diminishes you.
A boy loses his heart to Jerusalem
and dancers retell the story for generations
as every city is dispersed in turn.
No corner remains whose language

isn't language at all but a harp song
crippled out of its silence
because of the dry, expressionless tragedy on our faces
If I were you, there would be no harm.
In Jerusalem, there would be no harm.
It is the malforming sense of apartness

and of the tarred valley of death
that sets us on one another like animals.
The sky gone, the coherent succession
of bodies gone, and in their place
the abstract charity of power and remorse
hurts little wings and shadows and deserts.

Touch the book as though it were a tuned string.
That is not my voice or yours.
Travel a great distance and take
an expensive room. It is not Jerusalem
where our shadows had claws and did not starve.
A little, and then a great diaspora, this poor love.

Polygamy

Small operas, the seedy merchants
at the blurred ends of fuming streets
in the immigrant photographs, insist on it.
What are you supposed to do with desire
in America, where your heart is so many
poor shops? He takes a girl to the Catskills
on a bus. Her dull kerchief and the black hairs
wire out in sad profile against the window.
He marries her. He understands the milk-lipped
and clean economy in his hand
touching her hair. The plight of the stateless.
The hopeless milk inside the cool mouths
of the Baltic. She has so much to sell
across the little counter until it is all sold.

What are you supposed to do with scarcity
when you are starving yourself and the next street
is another America just as sad
with its own kinds of trees and with adults
living in a child's room, bowed under the beams?
I married a woman, knowing I was stealing from her,
knowing what becomes of desire
in stateless times and at the blurred ends
of streets and to the immigrant music
of small operas bowed under the beams.
Understanding the economy of love
fills no shop, liberates no country.
No one ever returns after he cheats someone.
He stares out bus windows. He walks
the cold margin of the Baltic, looking for coins.

The Northeast Corridor

The bar in the commuter station steams
like a ruin, its fourth wall open
to the crowd and the fluttering timetables.
In the farthest corner, the television
crackles a torch song and a beaded gown.
She is my favorite singer, dead when I was born.
And I have been waiting for hours for a train,
exhausted between connections to small cities,
awake only in my eyes finding shelter
in the fluttering ribbon of shadow
around the dead woman singing on the screen.
Exhaustion is a last line of defense
where time either stops dead or kills you.
It teaches you to see what your eyes see
without questions, without the politics
of living in one city, dying in another.

How badly I would like to sleep now
in the shadows beside real things or beside
things that were real once, like the beaded gown
on the television, like the debut
of a song in New York in black and white
when my parents were there. I feel sometimes
my life was used up before I was born.
My eyes sear backwards into my head
to the makeshift of what I have already seen
or heard described or dreamed about, too weary
not to envy the world its useless outlines.
Books of photographs of New York in the forties.
The dark rhombus of a window of a train
rushing past my train. The dark halo
around the body of a woman I love
from something much farther than a distance.

The world is insatiable. It takes your legs off,
it takes your arms and parades in front of you
such wonderful things, such pictures of warm houses
trellised along the sides with green so deep
it is like black air, only transparent,
of women singing, of trains of lithium
on the awakening body of a landscape
or across the backdrop of an old city
steaming and high-shouldered as the nineteen-forties.
The world exhausts everything except my eyes
because it is a long walk to the world
begun before I was born. In the far corner
the dead woman bows off stage. The television
crumples into a white dot as the last
train of the evening, my train, is announced.
I lived in one place. I want to die in another.

The New World

A little emptiness beforehand,
and then I take up the exhausted
slogans, the party of one whose single issue
is a house a little above street level,
the remote handiwork of the ironmonger
like a signature afloat in porchlight,
a place you do not have to carry with you
as I carry mine out of a little emptiness
into bad museums where I spend time.

Every man's routine is fantastic.
Read the transcripts. Spend some time
bent over the glass cases reading spider diaries
and opaque, absolutely usual daybooks
of the colonists. Obsessed with the familiar
(as we are not), with death in a spinney
or underneath an uncleared half-acre,
they recount nothing. And even nothing is so private
the handwriting crooks into scythes and obscenities.

In the next room, a handful of religious paintings.
A little emptiness in the faces,
especially in the eyes of the Christ child
staring away from His Mother.
Often, she was the painter's mistress posed
as Mary. She looks frightened, perhaps of blaspheming
or of being beaten by the rogue who paints her.
I stand as close to the pictures as I can.
The cracks in the paint flourish like handwriting

or like new streets from the air,
so much personal history dispersing
leaving only the false record of sentiment,
the old religion of the Puritan daybooks.
Life leaves nothing behind itself. Culture
is the traduction of routine
under the yellow light of museums, an emptiness
old and new, level with the street.
Outside, the remote handiwork of traffic makes no sound.

A Parish in the Bronx

The moving filaments of traffic shadow
the people and jagged, stationary cars
in a church parking lot below the highway.
Anyone leaving the late mass has a choice,
a lucky one. He can look up as far
as the highway and believe in so many lights
moving fast. Or he can look up farther
to the spire razored in floodlights,
taller than the traffic or the near buildings,
and picture himself that high, that visible.

Some choices are too easy to make
only because nothing hangs in the balance.
Coming out of the darkness of a church
into a dark neighborhood smeared beneath pylons,
nobody has anything to lose
between the heavens of the fast cars
and of the spire razored where everyone can see.
I felt so lucky when I stood there.
I felt like the last organ note of a hymn
huge inside of the nothing that comes afterwards.

There is no room between eternity
and the loneliness inside a car
and the loneliness of the floodlights cutting
a tall scaffold into the night sky.
I came out of mass and made a choice
lucky to believe the choice mattered.
The fast cars sped out of the city to dances
and marriages. The sharp spire
laddered upwards into the easy fame
of the last note of a hymn held forever.

I am no dancer. And marriage
never gets to the end of anything.
I chose the perspectiveless, tall nonsense
of God's noise aloft over the jagged parish,
thinking everything else was a dream
too lonely for words. It was, but just as lonely
is praying that all wives return, all dogs live.
Eternity takes up all the room in the world.
You can't drive fast enough. You can't picture yourself
so high that the dead see you and come home.

Perspective

The view from the air belongs to no one.
Those silences and fractious parklands
constantly retreat from one another
like ordinary people desperate for privacy.
The view from the air is of wounded lions,
of an intimacy God will not share,
the grilles and trellises of every death
uncommunicated in a big country.

Happiness divides us, sometimes
in God's name, sometimes in the name of History.
I could be happy now. From my seat in the airplane
I could imagine the full enclosures of people
contented and with no needs beyond
private moments walking the fenceline
before joining the others in the night enclosure
that is the final shape of countries.

I could be happy tomorrow. I could see myself
out in the dark all night and in the morning
standing upright beyond the fenceline,
seeing for myself the land has no shape
and is spotted with lions dying ignorant
of the airplanes overhead.
I would be happy because of the justice
that every death belongs to lions and has no country.

The grilles and trellises of the view from the air,
windows cut into a hundred pictures,
ladders of huge flowers disappearing,
make me think there is no such thing as the world.
The wisdom of God kills lions.
The undirected freedoms of History
kill lions. And there is a happiness in me
that cannot live on the ground or save my country.

The Night Orchard

They have given me a room near the power station
across the canal, and sleeplessness has become
an island jolted by hot sounds and water lights.
A vapory static scents the air like fruit
that has caught fire. Thickly, the shallows
of a dream that I would have if I slept
darken under a greasy skin that won't break.
And then the scent of fire again, sweet, heaviest
near a woman's letter to me, propped on the nightstand.

As you near the center of America,
you reach an unmoving inland sea of towns
founded, strange to say, on a migration
fleeing tolerance. The coastal cities
had accommodated small boroughs of affection.
Their harbors steamed with tenderness at morning,
and at day's end a borderless sublime
floated in the bankers' streets and you
might put it in your soft hand and then

into a friend's hand like clean money.
And so the undistracted governments
of heaven fled inland, upwelling
and lacustrine charters of orchards, tulip farms,
and in the next century, power stations
and bad hotels to afflict the transient.
Borne up and eddied in sleeplessness there,
in nearly a fever dream, I can sense orchards
burning and power becoming water again.

Absurd, because this isn't Florida.
They do not drive off frost with fires
in orchards as they do in orange groves.

Power stations do not spew forth shipwreck;
they light houses; they hang dry and solid
in their constant translating stammer.
But I am afloat somehow, and there is the sweet of burn.
What, if anything, upholds a person
cut off from the mercy of his private life

remembering the little flecks of burn
on skin where there had been no fire
but his mouth only and at morning patches
of white like sea mist? What is there to translate
at the center of America but roiling
shallows and, away inside you,
an answer to the letter on the nightstand?
The questions that we ask of the civil world
leave us one choice: either freedom

is identical with happiness or we are all
on islands in the middle of flat continents
jolted by the stammer of sleepless dreaming.
The money of countries must feel like a skin
or it is rubbish. I must be able to stand
in the center of the night orchard
and be touched by fires burning justly
in the good tolerance of the landowners.
I must answer a simple letter

with language wrought from my heart's error,
common to everyone by example, but belonging
solely to one woman whose body is sea mist
and whose voice over the telephone sounds so
much like wings that it must be wings
grown out of the flecks of burn along her shoulders

sometime after I left her bed
and she began to write such beautiful letters
addressed to hotels. Finally, the power of inland

cities must be a charter of the heaven
curled on apple leaves, small and perfectly
suspended between happiness and freedom
on one stem. As we come closer to a real sleep,
as we get that far, America is purely
and completely its center, down to the seas
in all directions. Its sweet produce
always afire, in winter and in summer.
The question of our civil lives stammers

between legislating the difference
and knowing the difference that sets
each heart away on islands, and it tries to speak
out of itself of the loving error of passion
which is the beginning of freedom
which is the beginning of happiness.
I have my answer. She has always known it.
I bury it and my face in her shirt. Great turbines
and little coins like new Floridas spin in the dark.

II

Since shee enjoyes her long nights festivall,
Let mee prepare towards her, and let mee call
This houre her Vigill, and her Eve, since this
Both the yeares, and the dayes deep midnight is.
    —*John Donne, "A Nocturnall Upon S. Lucies Day"*

The Judas Nocturne

Twilight is espionage conducted openly,
groups of unhappy men in topcoats peering
into ground-floor windows. How lovely
if the fate of nations flowered and collapsed
in little rooms at street level, rooms like mine
where I am just explaining to someone
that she is a cloud chamber of furtive stars
and that I have a map of them.

Modern times are an awkward spectacle.
On the one hand, our public selves compete
for scarce window space, for the opportunity
to see in to where power is decided
and used. On the other, private life
recedes like a glacier, a translucent corner
of heaven meant only to be photographed,
never settled. And each detests the other

even inside us. I try to tell a woman
I love her and can't go to bed with her,
afraid as I am of the least darkness:
my shadow floating over her stomach, the deep
pencil lines in her hair and in her eyes.
Her small chin falling to her breast
the way a spark falls in a cloud chamber
tells me that I am a liar and a bad man,

just as huddled topcoats at the window
and fretful looks the mirror image of mine
tell me I am the class enemy
of decent feeling, of the family troikas
clustered on islands of public recreation

in calm sunlight. I should go to bed with the woman.
I should find a hillock in the dark
and sleep until the morning when there is work

and nothing to be afraid of. How
can I explain that fear is the last, abused rite of freedom?
I fear losing her, so I must lose her.
I am afraid one morning I will have no window space
and no access to power, so I tell lies and steal things.
She has little breasts and wears a perfume
named for groves in Syria. My rooms
are almost heaven. When I was in school

I made a cloud chamber for my science class.
Inside it, the seeds of cosmos
sprouted in bad air, burned, and disappeared.
I never saw anything so pretty
until I saw the words "adultery" and "treason"
printed large in a manuscript about hell.
It was a clumsy bit of medievalism
but larger than the world, brighter than the end of the world.

The Inns of Protest

The airy, slow intercourse of a child, neither
real nor bodiless as all this green aspiring
out of a warm sequence of days in winter,
is what I would call "mercy." And beyond that,
the anticipation of solitude,
the uprooted hedge at the harsh end of winter.

There are so many of us.
There is such a thing as pride.
But anything involved with desire,
like a small wound, like the sexy emptiness
of the new jazz, reads only the one inscription
over only the one object of desire,

and prostrates itself before those feeble words.
I know this, and so do you.
Nothing is assembled from parts. Even the poor
winter is of one piece, all that wreckage
bound together in its rootless heart
like the gypsy names of the last war. As poor

a thing as winter is whole and loves just once.
You and I remember that we drove
out of a storm and found an inn
named for a mineshaft and made love like children
for the last time—slowly, not quite bodiless,
but almost. I call that "mercy," an inn

diving out of the dark, a shaft of light
as clear as the anticipation of solitude.
I parsed the feeble inscription above your eyes
and over the thin space of your mouth on the air.
Mercy always waits until the last time.
Mercy sees better than my loving eyes

because it sees the terrible politics
of losing everyone in the last war or the next war
or to their necessary collaboration with time,
that uprooted hedge. I am falling away
from a vision. The air is a child. The birdsong
is a music without brandy, merciless this time.

Tabard and Terrace

In a small town with a bad museum
my wife died and her hair changed to amber,
the color of the deep scar on her lip
shaped just like a bird, safest in my mouth.

There is so much that I want to believe
it makes me wonder. Soft fields ambered
onto strings of towns. Tabards of money.
The night she lost the color of her hair

and we sat on the terrace looking down
to the sad novel of people dining.
She died and no museum will take her.
Nobody has any use for amber.

In the place I live, in the sad novel
and poorly lighted exhibition hall
of that town, the fields, people, and money
are deep scars like birds, safest in my mouth.

Heliotrope: Years and Years
after the Revolution

The leveling weight of music and weather
closes the stores, drives the people underground
into cool rooms under ducts and water pipes.
There are ways to prove the logic of whatever happens.
In a movie, the darkness between each frame proves it.
In dreams, waking and lying down into the same dream
just where you left it proves there was no accident.
But music and weather, this dim life
of broken, half-melodies in the ductwork,
of heat swaddled in cold air but with the smell of heat
still strong, a logic I can prove on my own flesh
but cannot feel and cannot tell the woman beside me.

A moment of darkness between my hand
and the needle-fine mist of her clothing.
A moment of waking and then the pull of sleep again
where she is ten years younger, in love with me,
and has not closed her eyes once in all that time.
But there is no such moment as the air
pitches its cold noise into the heat and peasant songs
of June 12, a day of clarity.
I promised everyone I ever loved
wisdom. I know about movies.
I know dreams, especially where I am well loved.
But June 12 is cold, an icon with its back turned, ducts and
    pipes.

The stores will never open again. For the rest of our lives
we shall make constellations and gods
out of the guts of buildings and the stale damp.
Noise is music. Half-light is weather.
The heart of a perfect woman, the perfect state

is a warm logic that does not live long
underground. It is like the guitar shape
and rainy frontiers of a wife
so small in her clothes, so wide-eyed.
As I fall asleep, the grassy squares of a peasant song.
As I fall asleep, the patient center of a dream
gone black. The basements of cities. June 12 so clearly.

A Prospect of Youth

I see them all so excellently fair,
I see, not feel, how beautiful they are.
—Coleridge, "Dejection: An Ode"

Cutting the losses, taking myself back
through the triumphal arch, everything
waving backwards as though it were under water,
I really do arrive, and it does feel like being under water.
Shocks of green, little gardens in the shape of pennants.
And it all waves slowly enough, with that drifting
motion of high summer, of young men in Brooklyn
on their way to see young women.

Perhaps I'm old enough to see the connection
between passion and small landscapes,
between buildings and apartment interiors.
The heart trapezes on lines of color, the narrowest green
stem breaking the underwater of our youth.
I met her in the alley. She took me up
into the apartment shaped like a green pennant
hung in a corner of the shadow of a great arch.

I believe every landscape is an interior.
All are private and seek even more privacy.
The shaded alley of a hallway and the little cells
to one side with a view of garden
and the watery sculpture of the fire escapes
veined with heat and of green going to black
in the lovemaking of the young in each cell.
What they feel is on the walls and is sweet countryside.

Later in the night, nearly everyone slept
in one big room at the far end of the hallway,
the television wrinkling a kind of stardust
onto their bodies. Yet one couple was awake.
In the angular white noise of the bathroom
they made love again, and tendrils inside and out
blackened bottle-glass over the veined toilet.
They made no child and grew tall in secret, in that triumph.

From the Outside

Someone lives a much better life.
I can hear her inside the extremest note
of a violin piece smooth as runners over snow
or as the smoke detached from the snow,
the only sign of life in the distance
where a town should be, and in the town
a violin player whose untuned strings
make a noise like some richer afterlife.

Happiness vends a kind of generosity
that keeps its distance and wants nothing
beyond the little village and its scraping
a few notes together under the smoky, circling
winter light indoors. I was thinking
that I would like to be everybody
in succession, dying that way but retaining
the memory into each next life. I want to be unhappy

as the dissonant wisp of music inside
each person, unique to that person.
And I want to be sure that everyone
whines under the wintry percussion
of what I have done, of where I have gone
by going so far out of my life
for envy's sake. I am the suicide
of that Dutch painter. I am the nameless one

opening the screen door into the warm pastel
of a house in Florida, the slatted shadow
of the blinds distinct across the gold-yellow
carpet and the famous murder victim in the furrows
lovely and nude, the last sacrificial
innocent of the 1940s. I go
disfigured by pathos. I go
unconvinced and unmarried by that tuneful

scraping of the village fiddler. I was thinking
that I would like to be everybody
because of the isolation, this living
apart in modernity and love's cruel going—
bundling her sunny hair into a hat, settling
into a little sleigh and leaving me.
Someone lives a better life, and she
is my sister life, a chill atonality.

Magus

The few, the lucky, make their way
into the brown, trilling apartment that one day
each year becomes a puppet theatre.
Inside, the smallest lives imaginable seem better
in their domestic chiaroscuro and small wars
than our lives, our phone calls, our knowledge of stars.

One Christmas, I could not travel at all
for thinking of the puppets. I could not
step out of my house for fear that I would lose
the unsatisfactory hearth and spoiled love
that were the closest I had come to a puppet's life:
the squared circle, the crackling formulae of words.

I have not traveled since, and I have been on the phone
a long time, mending and spoiling.
I recite the perfect correspondence
of Madame X and the Hussar fallen at the gates
of Moscow. I make a sound like a bird's
with a flute held underneath my tongue.

Those who stay at home become savages.
They become birds. They become the fictive Beloved.
And there is finally no language for us who are not inside
that brown, trilling and candle-warm circle of the puppet
          theatre.
There was a phone call I never expected
and a more than perfect voice I could not answer.

This is the miracle of Christmas:
for one day, everyone in the world is a puppet.
The corners of the rooms dissolve.
I answer my calls and tell them
that love is endless and undiminished
and that I want to feel even their smallest kindness.

The children of privilege know who they are.
They love the puppets and laugh and cry with them.
They are inside that apartment I cannot find.
I remember the smallest kindness, how
it sounds on the telephone, sings in bed.
There is nothing it does not know about the stars.

St. Lucy's Day

All I can put my hands on, even
my face in the dark window over the sink
staring out to the fading yard and inside
to the brightening kitchen behind my face,
staggers helpless a little sometimes
and then is propped up. What's important
is to try to notice each thing and then
know what stops it falling too far to save.
A child could worry about where the yard goes
at nightfall. And I'm here worrying
about the kitchen glaring behind me,
wanting me to fall into the deep end
of the part of the night after supper.
But unlike a child and unlike
mute things as easy to pity as to fear,
I know something and have a choice to make.
If I fall, I can choose what stops me.

History is laughing all the time,
shaking the little bridges between itself
and islands of freedom, the remote tribes there
talking themselves into a frenzy, forgetting
the one history lesson that matters.
The present is easy. It hangs there
like a rough pendant in the shape of a house.
You press a door. Everything inside is too small
to hurt you, easy to walk around
in ideal floor plans—tract house, cloister,
brownstone. Even easier to stand
at the sink and to consider your options.
As the yard fades, is it too late for me
to stagger through the window towards the dark house

at the fenceline, which is to say the past,
those uneasy rooms? Or better to fall
backwards into the deep end of the night ahead?

Easy to consider. Like collecting
water in a stone basin at the end
of a garden, letting time discover
its own economy, conduct its own
half measures of rescue invisibly
as everyone else does. But thought is the bad
economy of the helpless who keep thinking.
It melts like thin ice in a stone basin,
disappearing from all directions into
its helpless center, the here and now
it cannot enlarge and cannot abandon.
There is no saving myself anywhere
but in the past or future, no rescue
but falling backwards or forwards, into the yard
or into the mixed company of tonight's guests.
Whatever stops me falling is my real life.
I take everything there seriously.

The dark house at the fenceline never shrinks.
Even as the days shorten into the skittish
rites of St. Lucy's Day, it gets bigger,
opening its crazy floor plan wider
for more things, for people I'd given up
hoping to see together. Impossible
to walk around inside there. And sweet, never
to be hurt by strangers in so much darkness.
The deep end of the night ahead is full
of strangers ready to talk into

the small hours, rehearsing what may never happen
in new words, brighter associations
of shadow and real flesh and the blue patterns
of a woman's tongue I could touch with my tongue.
Impossible to be a ghost there. And sweet,
never to hurt anyone twice in one lifetime.
So my lifetime gutters between two real lives.

If he is honest, anyone can tell you
the same thing—at any moment, on any
of the little bridges of crisis
shaken by history's laughter, anyone
knows enough to make the choice he must make
between trying to live in the past
or the future. And nothing more than trying
because the choice comes again and again
onto the thin ice we never completely
abandon. That's how important the unreal
easy life of the present remains in spite
of the dangers. If I fall, tonight I fall
but one way. The shadow and flesh and tongue
of a woman in the next room are not
for my life. The night ahead is too fast.
Home, which I shall never reach, stands at the fenceline,
dark, slow, and filling with days that will not get longer.

III

Départ dans l'affection et le bruit neufs.

—Rimbaud

Apocrypha

I don't know why anyone writes history.
The vertical, thin-ankled civilizations
of morning, the evening continents
just now taking their soft hands away
from the bodies of men killed in rioting,
from the close, deluded eyes of one woman
whose angels knew none of Paradise,
whose physicians put her body in the ground—
what good are such things? Where are their teeth?
The heart bites down and scarcely knows itself

or the small, coral woman beside me
who would give her heart to the map on the wall
more easily than to gods in love with games.
The hillsides just beyond her window flower
in bright patches more generous than laughter.
The air is a clean residence and airplanes
buoyant overhead. A man in the next apartment
types out the name of a lost continent. He types
the names of its kings and the long rites by which
they became kings. He betrays each secret

in its turn, and broken characters
caper to the margins of his page, not suffering
because he has suffered enough for them all.
Gods begin with secrets, as do kings and history
and the mistake of pain. When I am with you
the temples draw into themselves like evening
beneath bright patches of the mock orange.
Or they do not, and I am in the teeth
of the faithful on the temple stairs, thrust
into the ground with bad angels and bad physicians.

Their gods were too much in love with games.
It was too much like suffering, spilling
out of temples, multiplying
into the less admirable bodies of laughter,
little flowers the size of your thumbnail
dividing hillsides and the air into so many
loving fragments that the temples died
of increase. I knew a man who died in the rioting.
I know a woman who mistook those flowers
for the ascent of angels and pure physicians.

The World's Fair Cities

Too many people on both sides of a window
iced over in fronds, the light keenest
where it came onto the bed or went out
to the station platform below the window
at night when they could see us from the trains.

The point of traveling is to arrive.
Nothing along the way speaks the language
or has the history to understand
fast birds of gesture I invented
as a child and use over and over.

The little atmospheres of the night trains.
The ends of the line where I am kissed softly,
taking my place over the rails or inside
rooms overlooking the station with a girl
staring through ice fronds at the trains.

The point of arriving is to set free
millions of birds of hand gestures
invented somewhere between fate and freedom.
To do it quickly, because too many people
are watching from outside or right next to you.

Not a matter of the right words, but of nearly all.
I think that finding a center means talking
without a lot of sense really, someplace
you never thought to go or to remember.
Five years ago, I bought a bottle of whisky

and went somewhere I never should have gone.
I was so happy. One window the whole length
of the room froze over and the trains made streamers
of light and noise behind the ice. I was happy
and talked crazy with both of my hands.

Wartime

All the more beautiful in the concert hall
with people in their fine clothes and yourself
in the same place as the original music.
The rest, I imagine, must be like the sound
of a radio orchestra in the nineteen-forties,
Europe fiddling beneath the darkness,
and those abandoned in the capital cities
leaning into the sound as it becomes noise.

Our lives seldom advance. And the beautiful
is a principle either too large
or too small to contain so much loose
and indispensable striving.
That is why I think of music, why I love
even the idea of an orchestra
in the open spaces of the outdoors
and worried corners of rooms during the blitz, my love's
          last hours.

They do not move much, but they are real.
They live in the anticipation
and in the backwards aftermath. They feel
light canceling the illumination
of the previous moment when I told you
Europe was dead. Mahler already knew.
That is why I said that being inside of you
is the harsh Symphony and withdrawing from you

a song at the end, something of the earth
too large for desire, too small to survive.
And these analogies are still nowhere
close to you, close to me, who are trying
so hard to believe that things
are not the hallucinations of bad history
or of autumn settling into its long self-pity
of mists and overripeness apt not to change.

In early November, the city parks hum
beneath the thinnest frost. The couples
and solitaries have got it wrong at the
lake's edge, feeding the birds, saying
nothing to themselves or to each other
about the coming holidays, the anticipation
buried close by, in the wrong place perhaps,
but someplace. It fills the earth like music.

White Pastoral

It is not a film. You cannot stay outside it
feeling the actual breeze and scent
or play it backwards to the place where everyone
agreed upon a destination, a politics
in which no one is exploited and the material
for weightless summer clothes appears from nowhere.

I cannot call it death, although some would,
as they would throw a coin onto a map
of the night sky. The causeless stars are for sale.
Death is harder. It gutters between the names of things
in their stellar loneliness—a hotel orchestra
and a hopelessly late rose. White pastoral.

Out of season, only the elderly
and these others dislodged from their orbits
by marriage or the impossible deaths of young children
darken the shadows behind the palms
at night as the hotel orchestra
presses a tango against the air
where there is no flesh. This is the death
that whitens every smile and is patient.
And I thought it was too late in the year
for roses when one the size of a child's head
fisted through the snapdragons.
It wore the frost of October like a disease
and was four different colors. This is the death
that fractures white light into a finger splay.
It is not patient. It has no time.
And there was a woman pounding at the door
when I was in bed with another woman.
She was the palest thing you could imagine

in the vertical cold cell of the doorway.
"I am your last chance," she said.
This is the death that does nothing.
It is outside time, carries no flowers,
and if I had gone with her that night
my flesh would be the air in everybody's old age
and a shepherd would play his scrannel pipe.
White pastoral: the small breast of death,
the legs like a boy's, the causeless
absolute effect of light in someone's skin,
of sound inside someone's mouth next to you in bed.

It is not a hallucination.
Like a girl in an apron dress
running before her parents to the waterfall
where every Labor Day they take a picnic
and photograph themselves for the winter album,
it exults in the clumsy lives we plan.

I remember being told that no one
ever makes up an hour's sleep once it is lost.
You just go on, tired to the end.
Orchestras disband. Roses collapse inward.
There is no time for happiness, but I feel it
as I feel the weightless summer clothes of the material air.

Least Said

One little turbulence, a candle lit
in the hollow of a wall near the site
of executions. It was far too late
in the clumsy, ordinary hour of his defeat
for the invader to destroy them in any
order. Too late for terror. Time only
for the haphazard, panicked assembly
in the marketplace, and then the peppery
sounds and the bodies like incomplete signatures.

The autonomy of the dead is of no use
and has no memorial. It insists
that life is better purposeless
than committed to the bad devices
of perfection, better unremembered
than lionized among all the faceless lions
crouched along the remote spandrels
of official grief. The dead
accept no communion and rally to no sound.

That is their freedom. The fences and chiming poplars,
and then nothing. The buoyancy of redheads
in soft dresses, and then nothing. A hurried
sentence constellated in the pearly
accents of one rushing up a staircase,
and then nothing. Our freedom is that sharp line
drawn by the dead between a thought
untranslatable, asocial and the use of death
by thoughtless contrivers of memorials

whose purpose is beyond freedom and of no help.
We batten our days within strict limits.
Our small apartments contain less than we imagine
and imagination is a frayed thing stretched too far.
Occasional, generous lovers shimmer briefly
and in the small hours take to the stairs.
We do not call after them, or we call
too softly to be heard. Their sudden absence
is Paradise and needs no memorial.

Festival Tumult

Careless with the unhealthy orchestra,
stealing from myself the first thoughts
large enough to grow larger than the world,
I had too much childhood,
too many solos and fossils.
I summoned animals out of a toychest.
Like Adam's transparent zoo in Eden,
they did not live. Then came the wilderness.

No one is afraid of being stillborn.
In 1831, a boy was murdered
on a pilgrimage to Goethe.
You can see his outline still reflected
on smooth stones on roads out of Italy.
Not fear of death, but separation
from indistinction, from unmarked roads
through pollarded elms and vineyards,
the mess of pencils and genders,
draws the ivy up the wall,
the boy to the great man.
It calls animals out of a box.
But when they are distinct and the light
shines through them undeflected,
it cannot make them live against their will.
The wise child will find his murderer.

I do not like what I am thinking
this first hour of Easter morning.
Everything strains to be invisible.
The entire orchestration stumbles.
Faith is entertainment, an awful

comedian mimicking a child.
The last moment on the leaves before full daylight
burns away. Joy must have its way,
as must distinctiveness that made a zoo
of Eden and then a wilderness.

Production Number

All are frantic, like water flowers.
Dancing in the sharpest outlines they can manage,
the poorly loved, the compulsive
cartoon posters of women dancing at all angles
on the hoardings of cities in slant rain—
so many flowers in a tempest,
so many arms or fine legs broken to shards.

It must be popular, this crazy angling
for self-knowledge in the suffering of others,
especially of women. In the music of the 1920s
it turned the bridges of New York into arrows.
In the posters of Weimar it turned dancing
and beautiful women in repose
into bad engines, windmills of swords.

Ours is the century of popular death.
Our music keens at the tall centers of bridges.
Our poetry mimics the fast poison of dancing
because it loves women best when they dance
too quickly, their bodies the beautiful weapons
of the posters, of the bridges of New York,
of what it could love, groaning in Weimar.

We belong to death. It makes us famous.
Gershwin wanted to write serious music and he did
and the 1920s learned to use the bodies of dancers
as brass and drum and as a stamping chorus of engines
on the weightless, insupportable bridge of the next decade.
There was no next after that, and I can only
imagine what might have been, the same as you.

The Old Causes

In the cool future, one puts off her dress by a window
and another makes the choice
between inhabiting and admiring.

We don't live long enough to outlast history.
We shall not love with our bodies again
except in the coronal streets of paintings,

the unjust happiness of the ratty voyeur
for ones so terribly thin now
without the little flags of their clothes.

Great tyrants understood the flesh and our nostalgia for it.
The glory of the rainy square
The glory of oblique pillars
of sunlight on the tousled hairs of a bed
The glory of not taking you in my arms now
but letting the paradise of the next day
waken to find you already there
teaching me to live with no purpose
and the endless rain better than heaven.

I dream of the deprived utopias that may yet arrive.
I see myself repeating a kind of courtship.
There is a messy apartment
brightened here and there by the subjective icons
of a woman's life before I knew her.
Somehow, I translate all that
into the struggle and final triumph

of all of the people shouting one name,
and then it is my right to go to bed with her.

In the cool future, apartments and unfeeling icons
will face each other across our bodies.
We shall count for very little

or I shall have learned to make the right choice, tendering
the little flags of her clothes
between my hands like a birthplace

or the silhouette of my mother on the broken glass
of the apartment she died in
crowned with the future's coronal of lamplight.

Against Pluralism

Who will you point to? In the needle's eye,
or selling what you own at the strait gate,
who will know how to kiss you and just when
to pull the hair at your neck and say your name?
No single victim will ever be the last.
Not, at least, until one victim purifies
the whole issue of suffering
by crying out that his pain means nothing
because it comes from nowhere and goes nowhere.
The clusters of exiles in their storefronts
will be free then. History will end.
Lover will take her hand from her lover's mouth
and see only his mouth, not a sightless
fish's eye scored onto the sheet's marble.

It's a wise child who knows it is no angel.
The rest of us grow up hovering, visiting
our lives in the moment of pain or orgasm
or when the little fingers of pity push
inside us and we feel loved. Our suffering
gales beneath our wings like applause.
We long to repeat it, to explain it
to stay aloft and clear of our lives in that
mid-heaven of nostalgia and apology.
We hover over the camps, the forced retreats,
the ends of nations that no one can recall now
except as code words for catastrophe.
We alight for pleasure, touching the victims
as the hurt husband touches the bed his wife has left.

Father loved you with a passion. Or else
from fear of your long, inarticulate future,
he turned silent, edging into crank broadcasts
by a small radio on the screened porch.
Perhaps, as my father did, he moved out
into another house and had a daughter
with a redheaded woman who mistook his silence
for grief. My father never lost anything.
For years, I went to school with the daughter
as she grew fat and her red hair reached her knees.
Who were the victims? At what moment
should my father have cried out, the mothers
have cried out, or I have taken the fat hand
of my sister and walked off through the needle's eye?

And it's a wise child who can understand
that the mothers and fathers on the trains
see only the receding pastorals,
the lamplit villages of other angels,
and that his suffering is only one pinpoint
on a lithic hoarding of departures
each passenger reads like an advertisement of heaven.
The wise child goes crazy. How could he not?
How could he not be heartbroken to learn
that even compassion is compassionless, that it uses
the real or imagined pain of others and himself
for wings, for memory, for a marriage proposal,
for the cruel angelism that adores victims
and makes a fifth, airier element out of pain?

We recede. We recede. A virus finds
that place deepest behind the heart where it
unweaves itself into a pattern of false starts
like knots of villages and the one house
lightening at the crest of a green street
as its doors close to us. Dearest,
that is another crime of pluralism.
Hope, jagged with beginnings, scatters
our one real life among a dozen houses,
little illnesses of longing whose low
fevers contract the heart. You have but one heart.
And I have one. At the crest of a green street
we give them away. The night thanks us.
The fences shiver with cats, and the flowers close.

Feeling comes from nowhere and goes nowhere.
It is not a train. It is not one instance
of lovemaking or a lifetime spent together
running the dogs, dying finally face down
in the yard bed of herbs. We are all the same.
Or, rather, we should believe we are the same
in order to be happy with the same things
and not to be stealing from each other.
We put each other in camps. I crush my lover with a kiss
and then it is impossible to love her.
What must die if we are to live without barbed wire
and bad sex is the very idea of otherness.
And to kill the idea, we have merely to find
one victim in ourselves who will die for nothing.

My father could not stop getting children.
The people on the trains cannot stop watching
the passing villages for their own ghosts
and early angels. I cannot stop finding
houses in which to lose my heart a dozen times
in the fits and starts of a little passion exalted.
Life is not going to be bearable, I think,
for a long time. The exiles will play cards
in their storefront lodges. History will slide on.
And one will pull the hair at my neck. And one
will cover my mouth as she makes love to me.
The streets are snowed in under heaven's leaflets.
Our beds are scored with sightless eyes, the eyes of others.
The air is sickeningly heavy with applause.

New Dark Ages

The loose stonework and an outdated sense of freedom
like the word "airship" or like the fragmentary
sense memory I have of reading books in a cloister
on my birthday when the sunlight is always pure.
These things slip from the rail of a long terrace.
They fall into the street and past it, into the river.
And inside me, the airship lifts and swells
and people in turn-of-the-century costume
laugh with amazement as the loose stonework
and our lives fall as the airship rises.

I've never had much real control over things.
The music of pianos, for example, is the dead world
where I loved the machine of my small freedoms,
one of the crowd in his best clothes despite the weather,
the Eastern snow like the distinct sound of pianos
over the airfield. The music lifts and swells.
I remember this or that. And then a loose stone falls
and I am alone on the terrace of the longest,
best century, looking into the air for music
where there is none, all of it disappeared—
stonework breaking the surface of a river,
the lyric snow a thousand atoms of silence
skating over the surface. All I've ever done
is to wait, to gasp at the take-off and flight
of what I just barely feel. My freedom
as it was taken away early.
The sunlight stilling a cloister on my birthday.

The air is filled with ships.
A machine plays many pianos at once
and the music holds them aloft, a different tune
for each ship. Freedom has nothing to do with control
and control nothing to do with my weak heart
lonely for its birthday and the excitement
of pure sunlight and of snow parting
into countless buoyant shapes over the airfield.
A long, long century is crumbling around me.
There is much to remember, and I want
to give it all away, to become lighter than air.

About the Author

Donald Revell grew up in the South Bronx, "a desolate and frightening locale for which I still have a deep, almost erotic affection but which also made me feel a political and social anger." Many of his poems are about this childhood and the refuge he found in the beauty and music of a Bronx Episcopalian church. He was graduated from the Bronx High School of Science, from Harpur College (B.A. 1975), SUNY–Binghamton (M.A. 1977), and SUNY–Buffalo (Ph.D. 1980).

Revell was a National Poetry Series winner in 1982 for his first book of poems, *From the Abandoned Cities*, and won a Pushcart Prize in 1985 and an NEA fellowship in 1988. His second book was *The Gaza of Winter*. He taught at the University of Tennessee and Ripon College and is now associate professor of English at the University of Denver. He is editor in chief of the *Denver Quarterly* and lives in Denver.

About the Book

New Dark Ages was composed on the Linotron 202 in Trump Medieval, a contemporary typeface based on classical prototypes. It was designed by the German graphic artist and type designer Georg Trump (1895–1986). It was initially issued in 1954, in the form of foundry type and linecasting matrices, by C. E. Weber Typefoundry of Stuttgart. The book was composed by Princeton University Press, Princeton, New Jersey, and designed and produced by Kachergis Book Design, Pittsboro, North Carolina.

WESLEYAN POETRY